B.E.A.T. Bullying

Drafting a whole-school anti-bullying policy template

BEAT Bullying
Bronwen Strembiski

strembiskibronwen@gmail.com
Bronwenstrembiski.ca

B.E.A.T. Bullying

By Bronwen Strembiski

No part of this book may be used or reproduced in any manor whatsoever without the written permission of the author except in the case of brief quotations embodied in critical articles or reviews.

Copyright 2015, by Bronwen E. Strembiski. All Rights Reserved.

ISBN 978-0-9918305-8-9

Table of Contents

I.	**Introduction**	5
	Anti-bullying Template	
II.	**Background**	6
	Ramifications	
	Challenging Perceptions	
	Scope of the Policy	
III.	**Believe**	13
	Research Process	
	Primary Research	
	Survey	
IV.	**Engage**	25
	Establish a coordinating group or committee	
	Timeline	
	Financial Resources	
V.	**Act**	32
	Describe the Players	
	Create an Anti-Bullying Statement	
	Hot Spots	
	Training	
	Supervision	
	Preventative Strategies	
	Reporting Protocols (Systems)	
	Responding Protocols	
	Intervention Strategies	
VI.	**Test**	53
VII.	**Appendix A: Launching the Plan**	54
VIII.	**Appendix B: General Prevention Strategies**	55
IX.	**Appendix C: Charts to Reference**	56
X.	**Appendix D: My References**	57

Introduction

Commitment, collaboration, and consequences.[1]	Bullying is a serious problem. Having an anti-bullying policy doesn't mean admitting there is a problem; it means being proactive and clearly stating that bullying is not tolerated in your school community. However, not having an anti-bullying policy could inadvertently imply that bullying is condoned.
	The anti-bullying policy should clearly communicate your school's commitment to create a safe and caring environment. Once the plan is complete and implemented effectively, there should be an "unambiguous disapproval of bullying".[2]
	Unfortunately, it is seldom possible to have only one policy in place that will work for all schools and districts, given the varying working climates, student populations, and community demographics.

Anti-bullying Template

	The purpose of this template is to assist your school in drafting and implementing a whole-school policy to help you deal with instances of bullying behaviour and to increase awareness of the problem among school management, staff (academic & support), students, parents, and community organizations.
	Each school is unique and should ensure that specific references are applicable to its circumstances.

---

[1] (Field, 2007)
[2] (Focus on Bullying)

Background

Customize the plan to meet your school's individual needs.	**Name of school:** _____ **Address:** _____ _____ _____ **Phone #:** _____ **Fax#:** _____ General email: _____ **Website:** _____ **Contacts:** (include name, phone #, and email) *Principal:* _____ _____ *Vice-principal(s):* _____ _____ *Counsellor:* _____ _____ *Administration Assistant:* _____
It is important to include both full-time and part-time staff. If possible, you may want to give an estimate of volunteers or outside consultants.	**Number of Staff:** *Administration:* _____ *Academic:* _____ *Custodial:* _____ *Bus Drivers:* _____ *Education Consultant:* _____

	*Playground/Lunch Supervisors:*_____ *Regular cab drivers:*_____ *Teacher Assistants:*_____ *Volunteers:*_____

Your school district needs to not only be aware of your policy, but also support it.
 	
Who can people contact if they have concerns about how the policy is being handled within the school?
	Division/District: _____
	    Address: _____
	            _____
	
	    Phone #: _____
	
	Contacts: (include name, phone #, and email)
	    Key Point Person: _____
	                       _____

	School Liaison Worker: _____
	    Address: _____
	            _____
	
	    Phone #: _____
	
	Contacts: (include name, phone #, and email)
	    Key Point Person: _____
	                       _____
	
	RCMP/Police: _____
	    Address: _____
	            _____
	
	    Phone #: _____

Often bullying occurs off school property or is witnessed by those around the school.	**Neighbourhood/Community Demographics:** (All off school grounds: proximity to other schools, businesses, restaurants, convenience stores, public parks, sports fields, heavily treed areas …)

Ramifications

Look at the Alberta Education School Act, Provincial and Municipal Bylaws, Legislative Bills, and any other documents that might be relevant.	Legal Ramifications • • • • • • • • • •
Different cultures may not only deal with instances of bullying differently, but they may also be targeted differently. It is important to be	Cultural Ramifications • • • • • •

aware of culture sensitivities.	<ul><li></li><li></li><li></li><li></li></ul>

Challenging Perceptions

As you begin work on your plan, and even more so as you introduce it, you are bound to be met by resistance. This is an opportunity to brainstorm some possible perceptions that may need to be changed. Once you've identified them, it will help you define your scope for research.

	Perceptions **Denial – Inaction – Just another trend**
Administration	<ul><li></li><li></li><li></li><li></li><li></li><li></li></ul>
Teachers	<ul><li></li><li></li></ul>

	• • • •
Support Staff	• • • • • •
Students	• • • • • •

Parents	<ul><li></li><li></li><li></li><li></li><li></li><li></li></ul>
Community	<ul><li></li><li></li><li></li><li></li><li></li><li></li></ul>

Scope of the Policy

To help focus the direction of the plan, you should answer the following questions:

(anyone entering the school, at any point in time, including community groups who use it in the evenings or on weekends)	**To whom does the policy apply?** • • • • • •
(before, during, and after school – all the time, including on field trips)	**When and where does the policy apply** • • • • • •

Believe

It is vital that everyone believes bullying is a problem. It is all too easy to turn a blind eye. You will need to gain support and one way to do that is by showing the prevalence of bullying. You not only want to look at bullying in your school but also in the larger community and the media. Just because it isn't being reported, it doesn't mean it isn't happening.

Remember this is where you are building your case.

A simple first step is to define bullying; be sure to include the types of bullying.	**What is bullying?** Intent to harm ~ Repeated pattern of behaviour ~ Imbalance of power
The type of bullying can be broken down even further into specific acts, such as name calling, hitting, texting…	**What types of bullying are there?** (Direct, Indirect, Verbal, Physical, Social…) • • • • • • • • • •

Research Process

Statement of intent (what we are planning on researching, why we are planning to research, how will we be collecting data, what will be done with the results).

_____

_____

Collecting the Information:
1. Issues of Concern/Roadblocks (data storage, confidentiality):

_____

_____

_____

Secondary Research

There is no point in starting the research process from the beginning, as so much information is already out there.

Research protocols other schools have in place	
Study relevant resource documents and legislation: Child Protection Act, FOIP, School Act, City Bylaws…	
Provincial or National Standards	

A look at Results

	% or #	Notes
By Age		
By Grade		
By Gender		
In Canada		
In Alberta		
By City		
Other		

Types of Bullying	Definition	% or #
Physical		
Verbal		
Social		
Sexual		
Racial		

Find out what is happening in the news. (subscribe to Google News Alerts)	Cyber		
	Gender Based		
	Other (New ones found during research)		

Number of media articles: _____

Number of bully-related suicides: _____

Number of bully-related deaths: _____

Primary Research

It is one thing to know what is happening around you, but even more importantly you need to know what is happening within the school community.	**Who will you interview?** • • • • • • •

	• • • **What observations have you made?** • • • • • • • • • •
Examine practices from top-level to day-to-day activities	**How does this policy relate to the school's mission/vision and aims?** • • • • • •

-
-
-
-

Current Code of Conduct
-
-
-
-
-
-
-
-
-
-

Current Internet Usage Policy
-
-
-
-
-
-
-

-
-
-

Current School Rules:
-
-
-
-
-
-
-
-
-
-

Complete a school audit (student health concerns, absenteeism, tardiness, office referrals, previous behaviour reports…)	Have incidents been reported and or logged in the past? If yes: How many and by whom? • • • • •

	•
	•
	•
	•
	•

Survey

It's about finding the underlying dysfunction within the whole-school system that fosters bullying.

Participants need to know who is using the information and how it will be used. Given the topic, anonymity is also ideal. It is however important to know grade and sex of the participants.

1. How will the information be collected?_____
   Phone _____   Written_____

2. How will the survey be distributed? _____
   Email _____   Letter _____

3. Who is responsible for compiling the information? _____
   _____

4. Will you use an online template?
   From where? _____

5. Will it be done in-house or contracted out? _____
   If contract out to who? _____

What do you want to know?
You want to know who the game players are.

You want to know what bullying patterns exist, what types of bullying is present, when and where is bullying happening, and what is the severity of each incident?

Administration	<ul><li></li><li></li><li></li><li></li><li></li><li></li><li></li><li></li><li></li><li></li></ul>
Teachers	<ul><li></li><li></li><li></li><li></li><li></li><li></li><li></li><li></li><li></li><li></li></ul>

Support Staff	<ul><li></li><li></li><li></li><li></li><li></li><li></li><li></li><li></li><li></li><li></li></ul>
Students	<ul><li></li><li></li><li></li><li></li><li></li><li></li><li></li><li></li><li></li><li></li></ul>

Parents	<ul><li></li><li></li><li></li><li></li><li></li><li></li><li></li><li></li><li></li><li></li></ul>

Other	<ul><li></li><li></li><li></li><li></li><li></li><li></li><li></li><li></li></ul>

| | • |
| | • |

Where are the "Hot Spots"?

Location	Type of Bullying	Incidents Reported % or #
On the Bus		
Waiting for bus		
Classroom		
Hallway/Locker		
Bathroom		
Change room		
Stairwell		
Cafeteria		
Library		
Gym		
Outside on school grounds		
Outside off school grounds		
Online		
Other		

When is bullying happening?

Time of Day	Type of Bullying	% or #
Before School		
At the bus stop		
Recess		
Lunch		
Class Time		
After School		
Evening		
Other		

Engage

"Desire alone isn't enough". Based on the scope of the material you collected during the first process of the policy development, do you have the commitment and resources to effectively carry out and maintain a comprehensive anti-bullying policy?

Establish a coordinating group or committee

| Energy and commitment are very important. | **Staff:** Bullying can have an impact on staff morale, anxiety levels, and turnover. "The attitudes and opinions of staff members have a profound impact on students."[3]
•
•
•
•
•
•
•
•
•

Parents: Sometimes this is the hardest group to reach and teach. It is important that they understand why the policy is needed.
•
•
•
•
• |

---

[33] School where

-
-
-
-
-

Students: Give them a voice (bullies, victims, and bystanders). One idea, if you are not comfortable having them in with larger group meetings, is to establish a Student Safety Committee.

-
-
-
-
-
-
-
-
-

Community: Liaise with key players and form partnerships.

-
-
-

	• • • • • • •
Don't set yourself up for failure. There is no such thing as bully-free zone and zero-tolerance. All you can do is generate awareness, and reduce frequency and severity. Make the school as safe as possible, for as many people as possible, as much of the time as possible.	**Goals** • • • • • •
Try to start with no more than five. Make sure you are able to connect it directly back to the goal. **SMART:** Specific, Measurable, Achievable,	**Objectives** **To…By….** 1. 2.

Realistic, Time scaled	3. 4. 5.

Circulate the draft policy and consult the school community, with particular reference to school staff, students, parents/guardians and the board of management/trustees.	**Policy Considerations** • • • • • • • • • •

Amend the draft policy, as necessary, in light of the consultation process. Communicate the ratified policy to other members of the school community.	**Amendments** • • • • • • •

	• • •

Timeline

Remember there is no end date.

Put as much effort into the launch as you did in developing the policy.	**Launch Date**
It is often appropriate given the resources to introduce things throughout the school year or maybe over a period of three years.	**Introducing New Initiatives** **August:** • • • • **September:** • • • • **October:** • •

-
-

November:

-
-
-
-

December:

-
-
-
-

January:

-
-
-
-

February:

-
-
-
-

March:

-
-
-
-

April:
-
-
-
-

May:
-
-
-
-

June:
-
-
-
-

	Maintaining, Testing, Review
Make provision for the circulation of the policy to all parents and arrange to provide it to all students, including new entrants.	
At what intervals will the operation of the policy be reviewed with a view to amending it, if necessary?	

Financial Resources

This includes both tangible and intangible items.

Act

It is time to move forward with the implementation. It is not enough to just have written words, they must be put into action.

	Agreed Upon Bullying Definition
Based on your research this is where you write your agreed upon definition. It needs to be easily understood and leave no room for questioning.	
	Type of Bullying • • • • • • • • • •
These incidents should	**What bullying is not.**

be dealt with under the school's Code of Conduct, but should be monitored regularly to be make sure the behaviour doesn't escalate.	- **Teasing:** give and take - **Conflict:** easy resolution (no imbalance) - **Violence:** isolated incident of aggressive behaviour - **Slagging:** good-natured bantering - **Flirting:** playful alluring behaviour - **Froshing**: Criminal Activity often associated with "right of passage" - **Hazing:** expected behaviour to join a group - - - -

Describe the Players

It is important not to stereotype or over label people. The following is designed to help you better understand why people behave the way that they do, and it will be helpful when looking at prevention and intervention strategies. Depending on the general characteristics there will be different needs. You want to "clearly define the behaviour to be changed". [4]It is important to recognize that the roles can change at any time.

Targets/Mark

I tend to stay away from the word victim, because it implies that the individual is stuck there and has no control over the situation.

Passive: - Socially Awkward New Kid - Smart Kid…	- - - -

---

[4] Davis,

	•
	•
	•
	•
	•
	•
	•

Reactive • Vicarious	•
	•
	•
	•
	•
	•
	•
	•
	•
	•

| Provocateurs: | • |

- Professional Victims
- False Accusers

Other

Bystanders

Look at and address the key reasons they don't get involved.

Engagers • Reinforces	• • • • • • • • • • •
Encouragers • Sidekicks	• • • • • • • • • • •

- Passive Supporters
  -
  -
  -
  -
  -
  -
  -
  -
  -
  -
  -

- Passive Defenders
  -
  -
  -
  -
  -
  -
  -
  -
  -
  -

-

- Defenders
  -
  -
  -
  -
  -
  -
  -
  -
  -
  -

Other
-
-
-
-
-
-
-
-

	•
	•
	•
	•

Bullies

Look at the possible reasons and contributing factors to their behaviours.

Proactive • Aggressor • Radical • Serial	• • • • • • • • • • •
Reactive • Residual • Institutional	• • •

-
-
-
-
-
-
-
-

Verbal
- Trash Talkers

-
-
-
-
-
-
-
-
-
-

Confident
- Elitist
- Regulation

Impulsive
- Hyperactive

Subordinate • Gang • Paired	<ul><li></li><li></li><li></li><li></li><li></li><li></li><li></li><li></li><li></li><li></li><li></li><li></li></ul>
Other	<ul><li></li><li></li><li></li><li></li><li></li><li></li><li></li><li></li><li></li><li></li><li></li></ul>

	•

Do not forget that when we are looking at these categories they can also apply to the following relationships:

- Student – Student
- Teacher – Student
- Teacher – Parent
- Parent – Parent

- Student – Teacher
- Teacher – Teacher
- Parent – Teacher
- Administration – Teacher

Create an Anti-Bullying Statement

- What does the school stand for?

_____

_____

Statement is not:	Statement should
A Code of Conduct is a description of the school's behavioural expectations **A Charter of Respect** is a purpose statement outlining the school's commitment to creating a culture of trust and respect **A Slogan or Motto** is a simple, easy-to-remember, "catchy"	• **Mention the word bully** • **Provide a framework** • **Create common ground** • **Outline commitment to anti-bullying** • **Be feasible and attainable** • **Simple terms and easy to recall**

phrase to communicate the school's commitment to bullying prevention. **A Flag or Banner** communicates the school's commitment to bullying prevention in graphic or symbolic form	• • • • • • • • • •

Hot Spots

Bullying is more prevalent in the non-structured times and less visible locations.

Students need to be clearly aware of the potential risks and be very vigilant about avoiding bullying opportunities.

Looking at your survey results, which areas concern your school and what will be done to help decrease the bullying behaviour?

-
-
-
-
-
-
-
-

-
-

Training

Without training, too often people miss opportunities to help, or even worse, turn their backs on bullying because they don't know what to do.

It needs to help the whole-school community in acquiring the knowledge, the skills, and confidence to intervene and effectively deal with bullying situations. Training should create a shared understanding of bullying and the effects on students, schools, families, and communities.

It should be multi-disciplinary and continual.

- Do you want to do the training in-house? _____

- Do you want to go off-site? Where? When? _____
  _____

- Can you bring an outsider in? _____
  _____

- Do anti-bullying training programs already exist? _____
  _____
    - Which Ones? _____
      _____
    - How do you gain access? _____
      _____

Topics to consider:
Mediation, team-building, assertiveness training, communication skills, mediation, crisis intervention, self-esteem building, conflict resolution, cooperative learning, stress management, anger management… (possibilities are endless and may change over time and vary from person-to-person even within the same general category)

| Training In |

Staff	<ul><li></li><li></li><li></li><li></li><li></li><li></li><li></li><li></li><li></li><li></li><li></li></ul>
Students	<ul><li></li><li></li><li></li><li></li><li></li><li></li><li></li><li></li><li></li><li></li><li></li></ul>

Parents	<ul><li></li><li></li><li></li><li></li><li></li><li></li><li></li><li></li><li></li><li></li><li></li></ul>

Supervision

All supervisors should be introduced at an assembly and should visit classrooms from time-to-time. It is vital that students know who the supervisors are and understand that the supervisors are to be respected. They need to be seen as authority figures by both students and staff.

Systems that need to be in place	Work Responsibilities
<ul><li>Build a supervision plan that clearly articulates roles<ul><li>Consider mapping out school boundaries</li><li>Look at increasing "Hot Spot" supervision</li><li>Leave fewer</li></ul></li></ul>	<ul><li>Assign "watch" areas for each supervisor and one floater</li><li>Have walkie talkies for easy communication</li><li>Model expected behaviours</li><li>Look for and reward examples of prosocial behaviors</li><li>Follow-up with students or</li></ul>

entrances open • Be specific about expectations • Monitor quality and provide feedback • Develop a reporting system between aides and teachers • • • • • •	teachers if needed • Complete end of shift log • • • • • •

Preventative Strategies

                        Be proactive and realistic.

What are your key messages? _____

_____

_____

The idea of preventative measures is to stop students from going down the bullying path and to help provide them with strategies that will stop the incident from escalading. Affective practices should reflect the policy's intent of fostering a safe and caring school.

Before implementing any strategy it is important to stop and ask

- How will it help me get closer to my goal?
- Which objective does it help me meet?

Otherwise it is too easy to create an unrealistic amount of work.

You also want to make sure that your strategies either teach or reinforce key messages and behavioural expectations. If not, do they help change the unacceptable behaviour by in some way modifying the environment?

Teach You teach the behaviours - They practice it You coach it - they rehearse it	Encourage positive involvement in school activities. ● ● ● ● ● ● ● ● ● ●
Reinforce	● ● ● ● ● ● ● ● ● ●

Modify Environment Climate Enhancement	• • • • • • • • • •

How can anti-bullying messages be integrated into the curriculum across subject areas?

-
-
-
-
-
-
-

Do programs already exist?_____

　　　o What?_____

- Where?_____
- How do I access them? _____

What Resources Have we Made Available?

Is there a comprehensive list?

-
-
-

Are they accessible?

-
-
-

Is there a mixture of mediums?

-
-
-

Reporting Protocols (Systems)

The reporting process should encourage communication.

- Do individuals know how to report incidents or tips?_____
  - Is it easy?_____

- Is it anonymous? _____

- Is there more than one method? (random secret ballots, bully box, phone/email tip) _____

- Do they know what to report? _____

- Do they understand the next steps in the process? _____

- Is there one individual responsible for reviewing the complaints and delegating them to the appropriate people? _____

Who do we tell and how?

Explain limits of confidentiality and that everyone has the responsibility for the safety of others. Reminded that watching bullying or knowing about it and doing nothing means you condone the behaviour.

Another student	• • • • • •
A staff member	• • • • • •

A parent	<ul><li></li><li></li><li></li><li></li><li></li><li></li></ul>

Responding Protocols

Steps to be taken

1.

2.

3.

4.

5.

6.

7.

8.

9.

10.

11.

12.

Offering support

For the Target	<ul><li></li><li></li><li></li><li></li><li></li><li></li></ul>
For the Bystanders	<ul><li></li><li></li><li></li><li></li><li></li><li></li></ul>
For the Bullies	•

	<ul><li></li><li></li><li></li><li></li><li></li></ul>

Tracking System
- Maintain reports for future trend analysis and keep them confidential

_____

_____

*Appeal Mechanism:*_____

_____

Intervention Strategies

The strategies are often tiered based on frequency and severity:

- Review number of prior incidents

First Offence	Second Offence	Third Offence	Fourth +

- evaluate the type and severity of bullying behaviour

	Mild	Medium	Sever
Verbal			
Physical			
Social			
Cyber			

Test

It is important to check, at regular intervals, that the policy is being implemented and identify any issues arising. This means taking the time to review and evaluate the impact of the policy at a pre-determined time, taking into account feedback from the school community and other developments.

Who will do what and when to confirm that the actions/measures set down under the policy are being implemented?

_____

_____

Suggestions for review and tracking
Go back to your objectives and survey.

Feedback received	
School and classroom observations	
# of rewards for expected behaviour	
# of reported bullying incidents (include type and location)	
How quickly and effectively were reports dealt with	
Other	

Appendix D: My References

I'd like to take this opportunity to apologize if it appears that I have used your work without your permission. This document has been compiled from years of research and many items were lost or mixed up. If you do notice a direct correlation and believe I have violated your copyrights, please contact me immediately to rectify your concern.

- Elliott, M. & Kilpatrick, J. (1994) How to Stop Bullying: A Kidscape Training Guide. London: Kidscape.
- Garrity, Carla et al., Bully-proofing Your School. Sopris, West Colorado, 1997
- Lee, Chris. (2004) Preventing Bullying in Schools. Sage Publications (http://site.ebrary.com/lib/athabasca/doc?id=10218290&ppg=1)
- Rigby, Ken, Stop the Bullying: A handbook for schools. ACER, Melbourne, 2003
- Smith, Peter K. & Sharp, Sonia (1994) Tackling Bullying in Your School: A Practical Handbook for Teachers. New York
- Sullivan, Keith. (2000) The Anti-Bullying Handbook. Oxford UP, New Zealand
- Focus on Bullying. B.C. Ministry of Education (http://www.bced.gov.bc.ca/sco/resourcedocs/bullying.pdf)

Teacher/School Resources

- Beane, A. (1999) The Bully Free Classroom. Minneapolis, MIN: Free Spirit Publications.
- Besag, V. (1992) We don't have bullies here! V.Besag, 57 Manor House Road, Jesmond, Newcastle-upon-Tyne NE2 2LY.

Parent Resources

- Cohen-Posey, Kate (1995) How to Handle Bullies, Teasers and Other Meanies, Rainbow Books, Highland City, Florida.
- Coloroso, Barbara. (2003) The Bully, the Bullied and the Bystander, Harper/Quill, New York.
- Elliot, M. (1997). 101 Ways to Deal with Bullying: A guide for parents, Stoughton.

- Fried, Suellen and Fried, Paula. (1998). Bullies and Victims: Helping your child through the schoolyard battlefield,. M. Evans and Co., New York.
- Simmons, Rachel. (2002). Odd Girl Out: The hidden culture of aggression in girls, Harcourt, San Diego.

Student Resources

- Wanna talk? Call 1-888-456-2323
- Copper Beech Books, Bullies and Gangs
- The Ant Bully (Scholastic Press)
- Beth Evangelista, Gifted
- Debora Allie, The Meanest Girl
- Alex Flinn, Breaking Point
- James Howe, Pinky and Rex and the Bully
- Steven Kellog, Jungle Bullies
- Alexis O'Neill, The Recess Queen
- Prose Francine ,Bullyville,
- Mary Stolz, The Bully of Barkham Street
- Rachel Simmons, Odd Girl Out: The Hidden Culture of Aggression in Girls
- Trevor Romain, Bullies Are a Pain in the Brain
- Trudy Ludwig, My Secret Bully

Websites

- www.bullyfreeworld.com
- www.bullying.co.uk
- www.stopbullying.gov
- www.stopabully.ca/
- www.prevnet.ca/
- www.bullystoppers.com
- www.bullyonline.org
- www.kidscape.org.uk
- www.kidpower.org
- www.bullypolice.org
- www.redcross.ca/article.asp?id=24700&tid=108
- www.rootsofempathy.org/
- www.canadiansafeschools.com
- www.bullying.org

www.ingramcontent.com/pod-product-compliance
Lightning Source LLC
Chambersburg PA
CBHW081349040426
42450CB00015B/3367